bom
dreaming about you
and me
SELENA
Si vienen a bailar,
pues vamos a
amento
12
Como la flor
in love

Sing with Me

The Story of Selena Quintanilla

by Diana López

illustrated by Teresa Martínez

Dial Books for Young Readers

*S*elena Quintanilla rolled a tortilla and lifted it to her mouth . . .
only to use it as a microphone.

She turned *everything* into a microphone: spoons, crayons, toothbrushes. But instead of scolding her, her parents hummed along while her brother and sister tapped their feet.

The Quintanillas were always together—siempre juntos—
and they were always united by music. One day, her father
announced, "We should start a band!" Selena jumped up
and down. *What a great idea!*

Selena and her family began rehearsing their favorite pop, rock, and country songs at their home in Lake Jackson, Texas. Selena sang, while her brother, A.B., plucked a bass guitar and her sister, Suzette, tapped the drums.

When Selena was nine, her father set up a stage in Papagayos, their family restaurant. Papel picado hung from the ceiling and the scent of caldo and charro beans filled the air. No one could miss the giant banner with the band's new name.

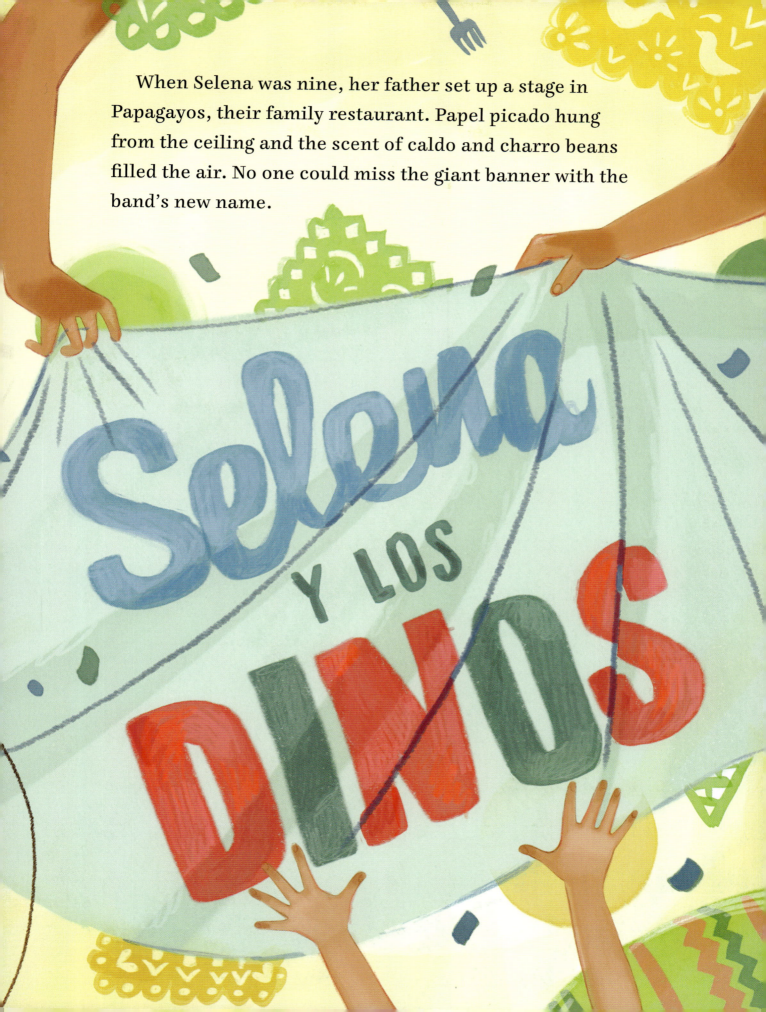

Selena
Y LOS
DINOS

At first, Selena felt nervous about singing for strangers. But as soon as she stepped onstage, she realized music quickly turned strangers into friends. When she sang feliz cumpleaños to customers, celebrating their birthdays, she said, "Sing with me!" The waiters, cooks, and customers joined her, their voices united by song.

Whether the restaurant was almost empty, or so full
that people had to wait for seats, Selena always sang
her best.

Then the recession of the early 1980s hit, and no one had money to eat at Papagayos. Soon the Quintanillas lost their restaurant *and* their home.

Selena was ten when they drove three hours south to Corpus Christi, where they would stay with relatives until they could support themselves again.

What will this new city be like? Selena wondered. She opened the window, tasting the salty air from the Gulf of Mexico.

As they crossed the Harbor Bridge, Selena began to sing. A.B. and Suzette didn't have their instruments, but they clapped out rhythms. Then their mother let loose a most glorious grito, and their father cheered, "¡Órale!"

They used their last dollars to buy a bus—which they named Big Bertha—and drove to Houston, Laredo, McAllen, Falfurrias, Del Rio, and Freer to perform.

They sang at weddings, quinceañeras, and rodeos, sometimes for as little as a hundred dollars. Times were tough, but at least they were together.

While they traveled through Texas, the audiences made requests. Selena loved to sing their favorites, but when they asked for Tejano songs, she found herself apologizing because she couldn't speak Spanish.

"Why didn't you teach me?" Selena asked her parents. They were quiet for a moment. Then, her father said, "When we were growing up, we got punished if we spoke Spanish in school. That's why we taught you only English. At the time, it was the language of schooling and success." Selena understood that her parents thought they were helping her.

But she really wanted this connection with her audience. *I'm going to learn Spanish,* she decided, *so more people can sing along.*

At first, Selena learned the songs phonetically, sounding out the words. *Roll your r's and remember that the* h *is silent,* she kept reminding herself.

After she learned a few songs in Spanish, her family booked a gig at a Tejano music festival. Selena loved the other musicians' bolo ties, cowboy hats, and Western boots. She was so excited to join them, but even though she said "Hola" with a silent *h*, they waved her off. "No room for girls in the Tejano music world," they said.

For a tiny moment, Selena wanted to give up, but then, she heard the music and the foot-beats of dancing couples. *It's up to me*, she realized. *I have to make room*. The main stage was for the popular bands, so she went to a side stage to perform. She put her heart and soul into each Tejano song, even when she didn't understand all the Spanish words she was saying. When she finished, she said, "Muchas gracias," and the audience cheered.

At twelve, she recorded her first song, "Se acabó aquel amor." In a room by herself, Selena missed the company of a band and audience. How could she sing without people to dance and hum along?

She closed her eyes, tried to put feeling into music. She repeated the Spanish pronunciations to herself and focused on the song's meaning, but singing in a studio was much different than in front of a live audience!

Then she remembered all the mothers, fathers, brothers, sisters, and abuelos who went to her concerts. She wasn't singing for the producers behind the window. She was singing for families and friends.

"Canta conmigo" she silently repeated, imagining the day when they'd all hear her recording and sing along.

Soon, Selena recorded more songs, many written by A.B., who mixed rock, country, and pop for their unique Tejano sound. Suzette kept playing the drums, and between gigs, she and Selena studied fashion magazines, designing new clothes, trying different hairstyles. Selena didn't buy her stage outfits. She made them with her mother's and sister's help.

Meanwhile, Big Bertha took them to stages around the U.S. and Mexico. Crowds of twenty turned to crowds of hundreds. On the road, Selena kept studying Spanish, the words like secret codes she unlocked, one by one. Most of the time, she still thought in English, but sometimes the Spanish words came first.

In 1986, when Selena was only fifteen years old, she won a Tejano Music Award.

She won the award again in 1987, then the next year and the next. Every time she accepted a trophy, she remembered all the people she had met through her music, and her family, the Quintanillas, who were always by her side.

She kept recording, performing, and sewing. She opened fashion boutiques to sell her clothes. She fell in love and got married.

On February 26, 1995, at the Astrodome in Houston, Selena circled the arena on a horse-drawn carriage. She wore her own purple pantsuit that she designed. As she waved to the crowd, she thought of her performances at the family dining table, at Papagayos, at the dance halls and rodeos—how different from the Astrodome and yet, how much the same.

Her fans cheered when she hopped on the stage. More than 60,000 had gotten tickets to the show!

"Bidi bidi bom bom!" Selena sang, then she held the mike to the crowd.

"Bidi bidi bom bom," they repeated, thousands of families and friends, their heartbeats and their voices united by her song.

That concert ended many years ago, but her fans are still singing. Every time they hear her voice, they also hear her joyfully shouting, "¡Canta conmigo!"

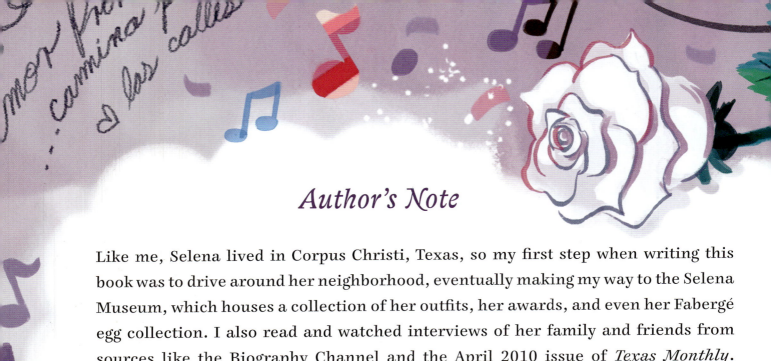

Author's Note

Like me, Selena lived in Corpus Christi, Texas, so my first step when writing this book was to drive around her neighborhood, eventually making my way to the Selena Museum, which houses a collection of her outfits, her awards, and even her Fabergé egg collection. I also read and watched interviews of her family and friends from sources like the Biography Channel and the April 2010 issue of *Texas Monthly*. Commemorative issues of *People* and *Newsweek* provided many images and much information about her career. But mostly, I watched videos of Selena in action.

I took some creative license when it came to imagining Selena using a tortilla as a microphone or studying late into the night. It's impossible to know exactly what she was thinking or hear past conversations with her family, but for scenes like when she first sees Corpus Christi or when she asks her parents about teaching her Spanish, I did my best to imagine what she thought and what she said by using information from interviews and from my own similar experiences.

Selena Quintanilla was born on April 16, 1971. Music was in her blood because her father, Abraham, had always dreamed of being a well-known musician. As a young man, he joined a group called Los Dinos, but they struggled to find their place. The Mexican audience rejected them because they sang in English, and the white audience rejected them because they were too brown. But Abraham never stopped loving music, and he passed this love to his family.

With her father's guidance and her sister and brother by her side, Selena started performing when she was nine. She would go on to win a total of thirty-six Tejano Music Awards. She had just started recording pop songs in English, including the Billboard hit "Dreaming of You," when she was killed on March 31, 1995, one month after her famous concert at the Astrodome. She was only twenty-three.

Thousands attended candlelight vigils in her honor. The Texas governor, George W. Bush, officially designated April 16 as Selena Day. *People* magazine published a commemorative issue that sold out within a week. Gregory Nava wrote and directed a blockbuster film about her life, and the convention center in Corpus Christi named its theater Selena Auditorium.

Over the years, I've met many young people inspired by her example. We talk about her talent, her struggles, but mostly about her kindness and humility. Selena never forgot her roots. She ate at local restaurants and lived in a modest neighborhood. She made her own clothes. She continually reminds us that we all have potential no matter how humble our beginnings.

We write messages—"The world misses your beautiful smile, your joy, and especially your talent"—"You're an inspiration to always be yourself"—"You showed us that we can break down barriers and do whatever we dream." We leave these notes beside white roses. We hum our favorite songs. We celebrate her life.

Studio Albums

Selena (EMI Latin, 1989)

Ven conmigo (EMI Latin, 1990)

Entre a mi mundo (EMI Latin, 1992)

Amor prohibido (EMI Latin, 1994)

Dreaming of You (EMI Latin and EMI Records, 1995)

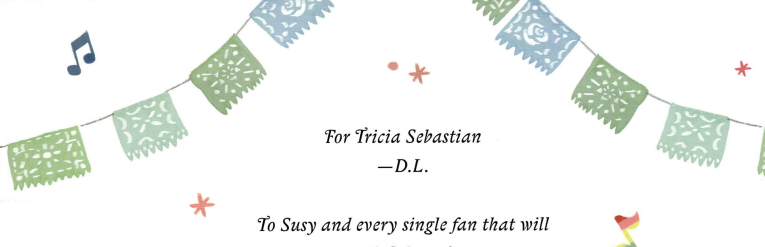

For Tricia Sebastian
—D.L.

To Susy and every single fan that will
sing with Selena forever
—T.M.

Dial Books for Young Readers
An imprint of Penguin Random House LLC, New York

First published in the United States of America by Dial Books for Young Readers,
an imprint of Penguin Random House LLC, 2021

Visit us online at penguinrandomhouse.com.

Library of Congress Cataloging-in-Publication Data is available.

Manufactured in China
ISBN 9780593110959

1 3 5 7 9 10 8 6 4 2

Design by Mina Chung • Text set in Cosmiqua Com

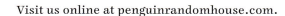

El
importa en ti
y en mi, ni en
el corazón
Bidi
Bidi
Si una vez dije que te amaba
En la esquina yo esperand
siempre su novia
se están burl